MW01277772

Fearless & Free

Being Brave with God's Help

Chelsey Dollman

Fearless & Free: Being Brave with God's Help

This book is dedicated to my daughters, Sydney and Ava: You both bring me so much joy, and I pray you will always know that your freedom is found in the Lord.

I love you.

Table of Contents

Before you begin...

* In each chapter there are discussion questions, as well as a prayer.

* You will notice some words are darker (**bold**). Those words may be harder to understand. You can find out what they mean in the back of the book (page 111-113).

Introduction

As a pastor and mental health professional, living fearless and free resonated deeply within me. I felt the stories, and experiences as though they were my own. The subjects of anxiety, worry, emotional health, negative thoughts, and patterns of thinking, are subjects that I am personally all too familiar with. Even within my past and current experiences of wrestling and grappling through my own emotional and spiritual development, I felt nudged as the reader to be brave in my willingness to explore my fears, yet in a way that I wouldn't feel alone.

Chelsey wonderfully crafted and articulated this learning journey for not only children, teens, and young adults, but I also truly believe for adults, as well. The value she brings to the pages of this book will greatly benefit and resource a reader of all ages. Chelsey's invitation to invite Jesus to be part of the scary parts of my life genuinely warms the heart and offers an inspiration of confidence. A confidence that is felt, and I believe, was cultivated by experience, and a personal relationship with Jesus.

My spouse and I of over 20 years, have had the privilege of raising two children, both who are now in their teens. Although our family is not perfect, we love doing life together here on Vancouver Island. We share many dinner time and late-night bedside talks around worry and anxiety. Whether it be around school grades, matters of faith and spirituality, making new friends, or moving into a new neighbourhood, we continue to intentionally have conversations around what excites us and what worries us. We choose to keep it open and honest, no subject is taboo. Sometimes we champion the dilemma, solve the worlds problems, and other times we don't—and that is okay, too. We embrace the learning opportunity at the table of every interaction in our lives. I thoroughly enjoy how Chelsey embraces these learning opportunities, offering refreshing wisdom through sharing her own experiences, and through the lens of scripture.

Mental, emotional, and spiritual health is something that I am deeply passionate about. Throughout my career invested as a mental health and spiritual guidance practitioner, I've worked mostly with teens and young adults; many of whom wrestle through the symptoms of abuse, engaged in substance use at an early age, and cope with pain in different forms. I've learned from our next generation that being heard, experiencing meaningfulness, and discovering purpose, among many other things, are essential to the healthy spiritual, emotional, and even physical development of our loved ones.

Having the opportunity of knowing Chelsey personally, I can confidently say she is a champion of faith through complexity. While the subject of mental health is often a topic avoided in faith circles, Chelsey beautifully provides practical help and tools for us to put to work in our own lives. Helping us address the tough realities of our day-to-day experiences through a spiritual lens that is refreshingly easy to understand for people from all walks of life, across the spectrum of faith. Anxiety, worry, pain, and frustration, continue to captivate so many minds and hearts, producing fruits, behaviours and thought patterns that often squeeze out as anger and/or sadness. You will hear Chelsey's heart for you penned throughout this book, helping you learn how to create new thought soil, reframe thoughts, and be mindful of the nutrients feeding your mind and spirit. She provides the practical tools and tips to help future generations as they wrestle and grapple with living fearless, reducing negative emotions, finding roots of worry, leaning in to building trust with courage, and boldly surrendering these issues to Jesus as he unlocks hope and healing.

Our families, churches, and our circles of influence will be greatly blessed by growing in our fearless freedom. I urge you to read this book and to pay it forward by sharing it with someone you love.

Chris MacDonald, RTC

Lead Pastor at BeLoved City Church

CHAPTER ONE

One Step At a Time

Have you ever felt like your worrying is out of control? Does it ever feel like everything around you is making you anxious, nervous, or worried? Do you worry about things like school, friendships, tests, doctors appointments, or if everyone likes you? If we know that God fully loves us, why do we still worry? Sometimes our minds can get in the way of what our heart knows. We can easily walk down the path of worry, and then believe that there is something wrong with us if we worry.

I understand the feelings you have because I have had the same ones. I wasted so many years of my life living in fear, worry and anxiety. I didn't even know what anxiety was at the time because no one had ever told me. My body would get sweaty. Sometimes I would feel dizzy or spaced out, my heart would beat fast, or I'd get a tummy-ache. It would feel like the fear inside surrounded me.

I am also a teacher, and as a teacher, I've seen many kids in my classroom struggle with anxiety. Maybe you've felt those feelings, too, and you don't want them anymore. Inside you might know that your fears seem silly or don't make sense, but they still feel very real to you. Sometimes it may feel like no one else seems to get how you feel because they don't have that same fear. Your parents, friends, or teachers may tell you to not be afraid, and it seems simple to them, but the fear you feel can be very **overwhelming,** and hard to explain. Fear holds you prisoner in your mind, making you afraid to do things with **courage**. It can hold you back from taking chances on things, even fun things like going on a trip or meeting a new friend. It also makes it harder for your family to help you or enjoy new adventures with you. They want to see you free from fear, and they want to help. They try to help you, but sometimes they are not sure how.

But, there is hope.

We can rely on the **Holy Spirit** to calm our fears. Do you know who the **Holy Spirit** is, or where He is?Before I explain that further, let me explain a bit about God and the **Trinity.** God is our Father and Creator, but He is more than just one being. He is made up of three persons: God, Jesus, and the **Holy Spirit**. We call the three persons of God the **Trinity,** which means three in one. It can be a little confusing to figure out how this works because our human minds have a hard time understanding, but here's a simple example to try and help explain it: Think about an egg. The egg has three parts: the shell, the white part of the egg, and the yellow yolk. They all are part of the egg, and they all work together to make an egg, but they are each a little bit different. Although this still isn't a perfect example, the egg gives us an idea of what the **Trinity** is like, even though it's hard for our minds to understand.

God is the Father, the Son, and the **Holy Spirit**. We cannot separate God from Himself. God is our Father who loves and takes care of us. Jesus is our Saviour; He died on the cross to take away our sin and save us. The **Holy Spirit** is our helper. It says in John 14:26, that the Holy Spirit is God and He is our helper: **"But the Helper, the Holy Spirit whom the Father will send in My name, He will teach you all things, and remind you of all that I said to you"** (NASB). He is God, just like Jesus is God, and He has special things He gets to do. He is with us wherever we go because He lives on the inside of us. He helps guide our decisions and gives us that feeling inside to know the right thing to do. His job is to speak to us, help us make decisions, and do the right thing. He helps us by giving us the **fruit of the Spirit** (love, joy, peace, patience, goodness, kindness, faithfulness, gentleness, and self-control).

THE HOLY SPIRIT'S JOB

Think about when you are at school and you get stuck on your schoolwork. Either a teacher or a helper in the class will come and sit with you to help teach you. They are your helper with schoolwork. The **Holy Spirit** is like that as our Helper. He speaks to us and helps guide us on the right thing to do in situations.

When you realize that you have anxiety or worries, the **Holy Spirit** is the One who will help you figure out what to do inside. He is the One who guides you, and speaks to you by giving you the right (helpful) thoughts, instead of the wrong (unhelpful) ones. You have a job to do too. Your job is to learn to listen to the **Holy Spirit** giving you the right thoughts, and practice learning to hear His words. The **Holy Spirit** is our helper, but He won't do it all for you. He guides and helps you, but you will have to do the work. If you expect the **Holy Spirit** to magically make all the worry go away every time you feel anxious, you will not learn the how to **overcome** the feelings of worry. It takes practice.

God is not the one to blame when you feel worried or anxious. It's actually your mind having broken or unhelpful thoughts. Fear does not come from God. We are told in 2 Timothy 1:7, **"For God** has not given us a spirit of fear, but of power and of love and of a sound mind" (NKJV). That means that God has made you strong and powerful, and He has given you the ability to **overcome** anxiety by thinking the right way, and the plan in this book will help you do it.

We often feel fear and worry because of something scary or fearful that happened to us before, and then we get stuck in a pattern of thinking scary or worried thoughts. Other times it's because we are worried about something in our future, but often these things are not in our control. Our mind then becomes stuck in a loop, and we begin thinking about those thoughts over and over. Each time we think about those anxious thoughts, our mind cannot separate whether it's real or imagined, and we begin to focus on those thoughts of worry.

A LITTLE GIRL WITH A SNAKE

One of my daughters loved snakes when she was little. We would often go on "snake walks" in order to find little garter snakes for her to pick up and collect in a bucket. She got so excited when we found one. My daughter and her dad would often go just the two of them, and she would come back and tell me stories of all the different kinds of snakes she found.

One day, one of the snakes she picked up let out a very stinky goop that got all over her hands, and she really didn't like it. From that moment, she made up her mind that she didn't like snakes anymore. We didn't want her to lose her joy over something she loved, so we would take her out on walks in hopes that she would enjoy finding snakes again. Sadly, it didn't matter how many times we went, it didn't bring her joy anymore. Because she had a bad memory from the one stinky snake, she believed they were all bad. Seeing them made her scared, and she would run away from the snake.

This is an example of what it can be like when we get stuck in a pattern of worried thoughts. Even though my daughter knew that she had picked up snakes many times without a problem, it only took one time for her to create an anxious thought about snakes, and it changed the way she felt about them.

She was little at the time, and she still doesn't like snakes to this day. Thankfully it didn't turn into a fear of snakes; it is more of a dislike. But in bigger situations, worry can turn into big fears, and they can change how you think and how your body and mind feel. If your mind has created a worried or anxious feeling from something that has happened to you, like a bad mark on a test, or a friend who wouldn't let you play with them, it can make you think

14

it will happen again. Once that happens, it is important to deal with your worry by talking about it to an adult like a teacher, parent, or a close friend, or using steps to work through it on your own (page 77-83). If you follow these steps, you can stop the pattern of creating more worry. That's why your body may feel those strange feelings of anxiety (sweating, tummy-ache) each time you see or remember the thing that happened. Not everyone has those feelings in their body when they worry, but some do. Others don't feel anxious in their body, but instead their mind is anxious, and they think about it all the time.

When this happens, your mind is actually trying to protect you by making your body feel things because it wants you to notice and solve the problem. Part of **overcoming** worry and anxiety is learning how to talk about your feelings and your worries with someone you can trust, such as a teacher, your mom or dad, your grandparents, God, your pastor or Sunday school teacher, your friend, your friend's parents, or whoever it is that you trust and feel comfortable talking to. You will also learn to set your mind on what is **positive**, and pay attention to your thoughts. Until you do that, your mind will have a hard time stopping fear and worry on its own. The sooner you learn to go through the steps I've shared in Chapter 6 to help you, the sooner you will **overcome** worry.

THE PATTERN OF WORRY

When your mind is stuck in a pattern of worried or anxious thoughts, many **emotions** go with it, like: worry about what happened or could happen, fear of the future, fear of pain, or being alone. Those are a few of them, and I'm sure you could think of something else to add to that list. When your mind gets stuck in anxiety, you should know that it's not your fault. It's something that happens to almost everyone at some point in their life, but the great news is that you can learn how to **overcome** it. It's your brain getting stuck in a pattern of thinking, but there is something you can do about it. You can learn to think a new way. Isn't that exciting?

Some of those anxious thoughts are our own, but many of those thoughts are lies from Satan. "Who is Satan?" you may ask. Satan is the enemy of God and us. You can't see him, but he tries to trick everyone into doing wrong or thinking wrong. In the story of Adam and Eve in Genesis 3, Satan tries to trick Eve into doing something that God told her not to do, which was to eat the fruit from a tree that God said not to eat from. Satan tricked her by making her question if God really said that. He also lied to her and Adam by telling them that God was not letting them eat the fruit because God didn't want what was best for them. Eve and Adam believed him and she and Adam gave into sin, and because of that, sin came into the world and their lives (as well as everyones after them) were very hard after that.

Satan doesn't want people to love Christ, so he tempts us to want different things than what Jesus wants for us. Satan likes to trick people into thinking his ideas are good. Sometimes good people can have bad ideas and they often come from Satan. If their words and actions don't agree with the Bible, then we can know their ideas are not from God. You don't need to be afraid of Satan though, because God is much more powerful. He has so much more power than Satan does, and although Satan can tempt us with wrong thinking or wrong actions, God gives us the tools we need to **overcome** Satan, and fight and win! We need to learn to put on the full armour of God, like it says in Ephesians 6:13-17:

Therefore put on the full armor of God, so that when the day of evil comes, you may be able to stand your ground, and after you have done everything, to stand. Stand firm then, with the **belt of truth buckled around your waist**, and with your feet fitted with **the readiness that comes from the gospel of peace.** In addition to all this, take up the **shield of faith, with which you can extinguish all the flaming arrows of the evil one.** Take the **helmet of salvation and the sword of the Spirit, which is the word of God.**

We need to practice putting on the armour of God to **overcome** the tricks and lies of Satan who may try to trick us, but God will show us how to **overcome** Satan. Remember, God is in control, Satan is not. God is all-powerful; Satan is not. God is **in** you, Satan is not. God will give you what you need to **overcome** Satan's temptations.

When Satan first speaks a doubt or worry in our minds, we may ignore it for a while or be unaware of it, just like Eve. We may think it's a harmless thought, but it's like a bad weed that gets deep roots. As that weed grows deeper roots, and as we think more about that thought or worry, it grows from a tiny weed to a large weed. That weed begins to fill our mind, and soon it's all we think about. It can be **overwhelming** and feel completely real, even though it may not be realistic. Our thoughts are there, but they aren't always true. That's because our feelings and **emotions** are very strong, and they can change how we see what is actually happening.

We do have a choice in this. We can choose to believe the Bible and what God says, or we can choose to believe what we feel. It's really not a hard choice though, because the Word of God (the Bible) is true, but our feelings can be untrue.

Choosing to believe something when your feelings feel different is hard to do. You are believing the opposite of how you feel. There have been moments when I wished my feelings weren't so strong, and even moments where I felt my feelings were out of control. Have you ever felt that way? Have you ever felt that your feelings weren't doing what you wanted them to? I think we all have, but our feelings and **emotions** are there for a reason, and with practice in following the steps in this book, you can learn to control how you feel in a good way. God created thoughts and feelings. They are what make us human, and they are not bad, but when we let our feelings rule us, they become out of balance. We need to learn to control our thoughts and feelings in a healthy way. You do have a choice in what you think about and once you learn to think helpful thoughts (following the steps on page 77-83) you will **overcome** anxiety too.

In this book you will:

- learn to pay attention to what you think about
- learn where the root of your worry is coming from
- replace the lies (worry) with the truth of God's word
- practice the steps until they become a habit

The truth you will learn and the steps you will practice in Chapter 6 will be your guide in **overcoming** anxiety. You don't have to try to do it all alone though. God will do His part, and you will do your part. It will take practice and sticking to it, but God will give you the ability, steps and **courage** to do it.

NEVER GIVE UP

A pattern of anxious thinking often first starts with hearing a lie or remembering a scary event which pops into our mind as a thought. Many times we don't realize what we are thinking about. Then Satan continues to whisper that worried thought and/or lie to you. Added to that, over time you may start to pay attention to what the lie is telling you, and as time passes you begin to listen to the lie. Often the worried thought plays over and over again in your mind. Even though the lie started out as being just another thought (many thoughts pop into our minds), it then started to feel very real to you in your mind. Eventually, you are believing a lie that you didn't even realize was a lie. This often happens without us noticing it because we aren't paying attention to our thoughts.

With anxiety, it seems like all of a sudden your mind can go wild. It's not as if you listened to the lie on purpose, but it's part of being human to have thoughts pop into your head, and to believe our thoughts and feelings, even if they're not true. Sometimes, the human side of us can think the worst. The enemy (Satan) knows this and he uses this to trick you into believing his lies. My hope is for you to be set free. Even if you did something or made a choice that made you fearful before, staying in fear is not the plan God has for you. God has a way out for you. God has given us a verse in the Bible that describes this:

> And remember, if you were a slave when the Lord called you, you are now free in the Lord. 1 Corinthians 7:22 (NLT)

Because Jesus died on the cross and took all our sin, we are now free. Free from sin, free from Satan's control, and free to live the life God designed for us. Isn't that good news? He has a good plan and a new life for you!

Being under anyone's control is not freedom; it's slavery. Satan doesn't want us to be free, he wants us to be worried and afraid and trapped in his lies.

> He [Satan] has always hated the truth, because there is no truth in him. When he lies, it is consistent with his character; for he is a liar and the father of lies. John 8:44 (NLT)

We have to know the truth in order to see what a mess we are in and to allow God to lead us **out of the mess**. Freedom from sin isn't something we could get on our own; we needed Jesus's sacrifice. In the same way, we need to rely on God to show us the way out of the enemy's traps, and into the freedom that God offers.

At the end of each chapter there are some journal or discussion questions for you to answer. I've left some space for you to write, but if you need more room, write it down in a journal.

Ask Yourself...

1. What kinds of feelings do you notice when you worry? (for example: snappy, easily angered, can't enjoy things)

2. Have you ever talked to an adult you trust about your anxiety?

3. What are you most excited about as you start this journey towards being freed from anxiety?

_____
_____
_____
_____
_____
_____
_____
_____

"Dear God, thank you for leading me on this journey to freedom. I know that with you, all things are possible. I ask for your courage to rule in my mind and that you would help me be strong. I am excited to see what you have in store for me. I love you, God. Amen."

CHAPTER TWO

Creating Healthy Habits

Have you ever been on a scavenger hunt? In a scavenger hunt, you follow a series of clues that lead you to a prize at the end, and with each passing clue you know you're getting closer to your goal. Thankfully, you don't have to guess where the final prize is, because each clue leads you to the next, which leads you closer to the prize. That's what this chapter is going to do for you: give you some activities to practice which will lead you closer to your goal of **overcoming** anxiety.

It's God's plan to give you the tools you need to **overcome** anxiety. There are lots of times in life when you want to do some kind of job or an exciting project, but you're not sure what steps you should take to do it. I believe the **Holy Spirit** helped me to understand these steps so that I could share them with you. These are healthy habits to add into your life. They are not steps to do one at a time, but rather attitudes and actions you should add into your life. Make time for them. I encourage you to practice them each day:

1. PRAY AND ASK

Do not be anxious about anything, but in every situation, by prayer and petition, with thanksgiving, present your requests to God. And the peace of God, which transcends all understanding, will guard your hearts and your minds in Christ Jesus.
Philippians 4:6-7

I love this verse. It's my favourite verse in the Bible. It says that in everything, whether it's a big thing or a small thing, we need to pray. **We pray, ask God for what we need or want, and thank Him.** It's that simple. I encourage you to memorize this verse so you can easily remember it when you need it. This verse helped lead me from fear to freedom. This verse is always on my mind, and I often pray it out loud. You can do that, too. I encourage you to print it out and hang it in your bathroom, write this verse on a piece of paper and decorate it to hang in your room, or write it somewhere like in a notebook, so that you will see it and be reminded that you don't need to worry. Let the Bible's truth be on your mind at all times.

2. USE YOUR FAITH

Jesus replied, "Truly I tell you, if you have faith and do not doubt, not only can you do what was done to the fig tree, but also you can say to this mountain, 'Go, throw yourself into the sea,' and it will be done. If you believe, you will receive whatever you ask for in prayer" Matthew 21:21, 22

In this verse, Jesus says that faith is the only thing we need in order to see the miracles of God. What is faith? Faith is trusting in God, Jesus, and the Holy Spirit. It's believing that God will bring you through whatever happens, even though you can't see it yet. Learning to **overcome** anxiety and be free is a **miracle;** it is not by chance. I know that God wants this for you because He sent Jesus so that we could be free. Have faith and try not to doubt God's power, no matter what thoughts pop into your head to make you think otherwise. Satan will try to plant doubt in your mind, but keep remembering the promises of God. Study the Bible, and if you don't have one, you could ask your parents or an adult for one, or you can easily download The Bible app on a tablet or phone, or get a paper copy of the Bible from many places. Read it lots and ask God to use it to speak to you.

3. READ YOUR BIBLE

> For the word of God is alive and active. Sharper than any double-edged sword, it penetrates even to dividing soul and spirit, joints and marrow; it judges the thoughts and attitudes of the heart. Hebrews 4:12

> Jesus answered, "It is written: 'Man shall not live on bread alone, but on every word that comes from the mouth of God.'" Matthew 4:4

Matthew 4:4 is talking about how the Bible (which is the Word of God) is what we need in our lives. Just like when you were little and your parents would give you the right amount of food on your plate so that you would grow up and be strong, God does the same for us. He knows what we need, and what we need is to know His promises in the Bible. We need to read them and be reminded of the truth. He always gives us enough to keep going and get through, and He gives us what we need at just the right time.

The first verse is talking about how powerful God's word (the Bible) is. We need to keep filling ourselves up with His Word so that it becomes rooted deep inside of us. Just like a tree needs deep roots to stand strong in a storm, we need our **minds** deeply rooted in God's Word so that we know what the truth is when the enemy comes along to plant doubt or lies. Learning and reading the truth in the Bible is part of putting on the armour of God that we talked about earlier. It's part of the "shoes of peace" that Paul talks about in Ephesians 6:15.

You will discover that the more you spend time reading the Bible, the more you will believe the truth, and the more it will set you free, just as Jesus says in John 8:31-32, "**If you hold to my teaching, you are really my disciples. Then you will know** the truth, and the truth will set you free." That has been true for me and I know it is God's will for you too.

4. LEARN ABOUT GOD'S CHARACTER

> The Lord is not slow to fulfill his promise as some count slowness, but is patient toward you, not wishing that any should perish, but that all should reach repentance. 2 Peter 3:9

This verse talks about how God is patient with you, and that He understands how hard it is. He has grace for you. Do you know what grace is? It's when we are blessed with something we don't deserve, like when you win an amazing gift in a contest or someone forgives you when you said something hurtful to them. That's grace. The grace that God gives you is that He took your sin and gave you a new life in Him, but He also is patient in helping you to understand how to live life in a way that pleases God. He knows how much you hurt, and He understands the hard things you go through, because when He was on earth, He felt all the things humans feel. He was still the Son of God, but He was also a human. Here are a few verses that help you learn about who God is. It also helps you learn about who you are because of Jesus being in your heart.

> But whoever is united with the Lord is one with him in spirit.
> 1 Corinthians 6:17

> Every good gift and every perfect gift is from above, coming down from the Father of lights. James 1:17

> So God created mankind in his own image, in the image of God he created them; male and female he created them. Genesis 1:27

> Jesus Christ is the same yesterday and today and forever. Hebrews 13:8

If we confess our sins, he is faithful and just to forgive us our sins and to cleanse us from all unrighteousness. 1 John 1:9

This God—his way is perfect; the word of the LORD proves true; he is a shield for all those who take refuge in him. Psalm 18:30 (ESV)

No temptation has overtaken you that is not common to man. God is faithful, and he will not let you be tempted beyond your ability, but with the temptation he will also provide the way of escape, that you may be able to endure it. 1 Corinthians 10:13 (ESV)

These are only a few verses, but there are many more you can search through the Bible App (YouVersion), an online Bible, or a paper Bible with a concordance in the back. A devotional book is another great way to study!

5. FINDING THE ROOT

A big part of **overcoming** anxiety, worry, and fear is figuring out where the fear came from. This may be something you want to ask a parent, teacher, counsellor, or someone you trust to help you with. Understanding where your fear comes from is an important part of becoming free from it.

When I was asking God for help with my anxiety, I would ask Him to show me what was causing my anxiety. I would simply begin by praying and asking God to show me where my worry was coming from and thanking Him. I would pray something like, "God, I am feeling worried, but I know that you want to set me free from that. Please show me what I'm worrying about so I can deal with it. Thank you." Then I would wait for an answer. Sometimes He would bring a situation or a picture to my mind, and other times I would feel an idea in my heart. It was never a voice that I heard, but I know God speaks in many different ways to many people. Sometimes it's through a verse or a song, a devotion or a friend, and sometimes it's a knowing that you get in your heart. He was so gentle with me, and He always dealt with me in a way that I felt safe, and I know He will do the same for you.

You may think your worry is about the thing you're worrying about, like for example, taking tests. You may think it's because you're worried about tests, but likely that worry is more about being afraid of disappointment or not getting a good mark. The test is what is making you anxious, but the reason behind it is different. Does that make sense?

I like to think about it like when you have a tummy-ache. You would probably try to find an adult and tell them so they could help. When they are trying to help, would they put a bandaid on your tummy? Of course not! A bandaid will not help your tummy-ache because it's not the right solution. In the same way, what you're afraid of or worrying about might not be what the real problem is. It's important to figure out what the reason is behind your worry and anxious thoughts so you can use the right solution to help. You will learn more about this in Chapter 6.

Read through these verses to give you hope that God will help you through this:

The heart of man plans his way, but
the LORD establishes his steps.
Proverbs 16:9 (ESV)

> Trust in the Lord with all your heart and lean not on your own understanding; in all your ways submit to him, and he will make your paths straight. Proverbs 3:5-6

> But those who hope in the LORD will renew their **strength**. They will soar on wings like eagles; they will run and not grow weary, they will walk and not be faint." Isaiah 40:31

It says in 1 Peter 5:8 that Satan is always looking to make trouble for someone.

He knows where we are weak or strong. He will tempt you to lose your trust or your faith in God by using your **weaknesses** against you. He will tempt you to question God's plan and God's will for you. He doesn't want you to trust in God, because he knows God has amazing plans for you.

You may be asking yourself, "That's great that you are saying

I can have freedom, but how? How can I move forward when right now I feel nothing but fear?" I've asked those same questions! When you're in the middle of feeling fear, the last thing you want to do or feel you can do is be **brave**. You may want to shrink back and tip-toe your way into the shadows, but that's exactly when you need to choose to be bold. You CAN do it! Believe the truth, and follow the steps in this book. If you practice them, you will see your mind being renewed with faith. Through practicing the steps, you will replace the lies with the truth. If I can do it, you can do it, because God helps all who ask Him and that includes you (see John 14:14). We can do all things through Christ who gives us strength (Philippians 4:13).

Every day and every moment, we are so blessed by God's love. He loves us so much that He won't leave us stuck in the mess around us. He is always working on us to be better than we used to be, and He promises to continue to work on you until it's finished (Philippians 1:6).

Ask Yourself...

1. Which of the five steps do you think you will find most helpful in keeping your mind on God instead of your worries?

2. Which of the verses in this chapter jumped out at you the most? Write it down.

3. In what areas have you listened to lies from Satan?

"Dear God, please help these verses to become very real to me, and to help me to learn to be strong and brave. I pray that you would take away my fears and teach me your ways. I pray for peace. Thank you for your help. Amen."

CHAPTER THREE

How to Trust God

Have you ever watched a sleepy cat enjoy its long rest? It often parks itself near a sunny window, and takes a big, long stretch before curling up in a ball and letting out a big sigh. Cats are great sleepers and they don't feel at all guilty or worried about taking the time to rest. They just accept that it's part of life and happily snuggle into their comfy spot to drift off into a restful sleep.

Resting in God is so important when **overcoming** anxiety because rest allows us to shut out the noise and distractions of the world, and focus on God. That is when we hear truth from God. Resting in God is very similar to trusting in God. If you think back to when your anxiety started, what comes to mind? Was it related to a lie that you believed? Was it due to a fearful situation?

Our feelings are not always honest with us, and when we see that our thoughts are because of a lie we believed we can then face our fears and learn the truth.

Here's a question I want you think and pray about: Do you trust God?

If your answer is yes (you do trust God 100%) then I believe that will help you move through the steps with more ease. If your answer is no, this is going to be an area that you will need to pray about and begin to renew your mind in. Pray and be honest with God about how you feel. Ask the **Holy Spirit** to help you trust God. Trust that He will speak to you, because He always does. Remember God's faithfulness to all His people in the Bible, and how He's taken care of you all these years! Trusting God might take some time to really understand, but God says what we ask for, we will receive (Matthew 7:7), so keep going and don't give up.

Trusting in God is one of the most important things you can do to walk the path to freedom from anxiety. The second is having faith that God will get you through the hard stuff.

I know that not trusting God was a big part of my struggle. I would worry when something came up out of my control, or when I saw things happen to others. I was relying on myself far more than I was relying on God, and it led me to a place of fear. I thought I needed to take care of myself. I didn't realize God wanted me to give my worries and problems to Him. I didn't know that I didn't have to figure it out on my own, but instead I could give it to God. The root (the lie I believed) behind my anxiety was that was I didn't trust God to take care of me. Once I believed that, anxiety began to creep into many areas of my life. Once I dealt with the root (the lie) and replaced those lies with the truth and practiced that, I began to have victory over fear.

THE SOLUTION IS ALWAYS THE SAME

The solution is the same for all our struggles with fear: Push forward as you trust in God. Trust that He is taking care of you. Trust God that He has your answer and that He's working it out, right **now**. He is working in the unseen realm to bring a victory that is better than you could ever ask, or imagine. Do you believe that with your heart, mind, soul and **strength**? Trust is something we all struggle with at some point, but you need to figure out what area you're having a hard time trusting God in. Is it lack of trust that He's taking care of you, like I struggled with? Lack of trust for a situation? Lack of trust that He is good? You need to dig down into what the root cause is.

I now know that trust is something I had a hard time with for many years, specifically trusting that God would take care of me. I didn't even know I had struggled with it. I hadn't given it much thought. Then, one day I heard a sermon where the preacher said, "Either you trust God, or you don't. Ask yourself: Do I trust God, or don't I?"

It was then that I realized that I hadn't fully been trusting God, and that part of my struggle with anxiety was because of not trusting in God. I had trusted God in many areas of my life, but I still held onto control in other areas. I had a little plan in my back pocket just in case He didn't do it the way I wanted Him to.

I would trust Him most of the way in one area, but there was a little part of me that was unsure, which created fear and led to trying to gain control in that area. As I began to look at different areas of my life, I realized that I wasn't fully putting my trust in God. Part of that was because I was afraid. The enemy had spent so much time whispering worries in my ear that I began to believe them. They weren't true, but they **convinced** me just enough to seem true. The hard part is if you believe a lie that you don't know is a lie, it feels true to you. We often let thoughts pop into our heads without questioning if they're true or not.

SURRENDER AND PRACTICE

Do you know what **surrender** means? It means when you give something to someone by your own will or your own choice. It's not something that someone takes from you, but something you agree to give to them. In this case, you're giving God your problem and all the feelings of worry that come with it.

A helpful thing you can do is to imagine in your mind that you are handing God the problem. Or you can imagine in your mind that you're giving Him the burden off your shoulders and giving it to Him to take care of. Or you can write it down on a piece of paper and have a little box or container that you put it in, kind of like mailing it to God. Sometimes that's really helpful because we can choose it in our hearts, but the physical action of putting it in your little box can help remind you that you've already given it to Him, and that it's not your problem anymore.

Once you give it to Him, you have to leave it with Him. Even once you've given it to him, and really made that decision in your heart, there will still be times when the worry or problem might pop back into your head without you wanting it to. Don't be afraid. That doesn't mean you are failing, it means that you're learning to put those thoughts away when they come up. It takes practice. How do you learn to put those thoughts away? If a worry or thought that you've already prayed about pops back into your mind, practice the steps on page 77-83.

All of these things will be so helpful for you when those pesky thoughts pop back into your head, and we will talk about them more in Chapter 6. Over time, by practicing thinking the right way (trusting in God to take care of your problems and remembering you've given them to Him), it will start to become easier and even become a habit to think this way. You will be surprised how much it will help you keep your mind on the right things instead of the wrong ones.

Anxiety is mostly about your thoughts. We often don't realize how much we think about things in the day, but don't stop to realize what we are thinking about. This is where worries and fears can creep in, because once you think about something enough, you start to believe it. The only way to start to see a change in your thinking is to practice thinking the right things, and by doing that you will begin creating new **positive** thinking habits in your mind. It won't happen in one day or two days or even a week. It will take time and practice, but please don't give up! I promise it will get easier, and you will start to become much happier as you see that you can trust in God instead of being afraid.

Do you remember when you learned to read or write or ride a bike? Like most of us, it didn't happen in one day. It took practice and time in order for you to learn how to do it, but because you kept practicing and doing it, you finally got it, and it became a habit. You can now do it without really thinking about it. The same can happen with your thoughts. The more you practice and continue doing it, the more you will see that it gets easier to think positively, and you can learn to trust in God to take care of the problems that come up in life.

Sometimes others may see your problem as little, but when you're anxious, you see the problem much differently. It seems big to you, and by others telling you it's not big and not to worry, it likely won't change your mind because you believe it **is** a big problem. When you're worried, you don't think clearly. Thankfully, when you start to practice giving your worries and problems to God and keeping your thoughts on the **positive**, a new thing can happen! When new problems come up (because there will be new ones from time to time), you will begin to see that you don't feel the new problem is as big as you thought it was going to be. You will see that you look at new problems in a much more relaxed and **positive** way. That will be an exciting day for you because it means you've grown from worrying, to learning to trust God, and also seeing things more clearly, and positively.

ASK GOD FOR HELP

Do you think you could carry the actual world on your back? Of course not! I know that in the past, before I learned how to think positively and trust God, I worried many times about things that were out of my control. I would be worried to the point of becoming anxious, but even with all that worry, it didn't solve any of my problems. It wasn't until I started to practice thinking the right way that I learned that the root of all fear is from Satan, and often he will tell us in some way that God isn't taking care of us, which creates worry. But when you think about it, God not only created the entire world and everything in it, but He is also in charge and in control. Once I realized that, it made it so much easier to give my problems and worries to Him. I then wondered why I had been trying to do it myself for so long when I could instead give it to God to take care of!

Faith is also one of the areas in which we often struggle if we are dealing with worry and anxiety. Faith is not only hope and trusting in God without seeing it happen, but it's also about believing that He will do what is best for you. Faith is knowing that God is real and that He has a good plan for your life.

> Now faith is the reality of what is
> hoped for, the proof of what is not
> seen. Hebrews 11:1 (CSB)

Have you ever read Hebrews, chapter 11? If you haven't, you should right now! It's such an exciting chapter to read about faith, and about the amazing things that God did because of the faith of Noah, Abraham, and many others. It helps remind us that we can have hope in what God can do with our own faith.

It encourages me that if the heroes of the Bible can believe in things that seemed impossible to man, like walking into a fiery furnace or building an ark when they hadn't seen rain in years, then I can have faith to trust that God will take care of my problems, too. I can have faith that I will get stronger in **overcoming** fear and worry. I can have faith that God will take care of anything and everything I give to Him.

I often picture God as my Shepherd, taking me (the lamb) and wrapping me around His shoulders as He carries me, like this parable:

Then Jesus told them this parable: "Suppose one of you has a hundred sheep and loses one of them. Doesn't he leave the ninety-nine in the open country and go after the lost sheep until he finds it? And

And when he finds it, he joyfully puts it on his shoulders and goes home. Then he calls his friends and neighbors together and says, "Rejoice with me; I have found my lost sheep." I tell you that in the same way there will be more rejoicing in heaven over one sinner who repents than over ninety-nine righteous persons who do not need to **repent.** Luke 15:3-7

This is a beautiful picture of what God does for us, as Jesus tells us. You will have some work to do, too, like choosing to control your thoughts, choosing what you will allow in your mind, and making the choice to trust. Thank the Lord that He is so patient, so merciful, generous, gracious, and kind to us. He is gentle. Our Heavenly Father stands with open arms, ready to help and hold you. He will lead you, hand-in-hand, on the path that leads to freedom.

Ask Yourself...

1. Do you believe you fully trust in God? What makes you believe you do or don't?

2. Write down the steps above for when a worry pops into your mind.

3. What stood out to you in Hebrews 11?

50

"Dear God, thank you for faith. Thank you that I have the truth of the Bible to help guide me Help me to trust in you more every day, and in every way. I know you are with me, but please help me to remember and be full of courage. Amen."

CHAPTER FOUR

Keep Going, Don't Quit!

When I was a young girl, my family and I left the comfort of the little island we called home and took off for a big adventure on a trip across most of Canada. It was exciting in many ways because I was excited to see my cousins and family that we didn't get to see often. I had cousins I hadn't even met yet. On the other hand, I knew the journey to get to Saskatchewan from Vancouver Island was going to be very long, and that it would test my patience being crammed in a small car for many days on end. I have two sisters and there were only three seats in the back of our very crammed, little car. It was a squishy, hot, and long trip only one hour into it! It seemed that by a few hours into the trip, we already had enough of each other: "She's too close to me!" one would say.

"She's breathing too loud," piped the other.

"Are we there yet?" I would ask, hoping that my question would be met with a yes but it mostly came back with a "No, and stop asking!"

When you are going through something hard, all you want to do is get past the hard part and get to the good part. We often need reminders that we can get through it and that we will get there, although it doesn't ever seem to come fast enough. It can feel like a long journey to **overcome** anxiety, but God isn't going to leave you in your anxiety, or your fear. He wants to help you! Sometimes He does that through **miraculous** healing, but most often He works with us, showing us which steps to take.

Instead of letting your pains, worries and anxiety win, you can let God heal your heart. Each problem that we **overcome** in our minds makes us stronger. Sometimes we don't understand why problems come, but we do know that God can work them out for our good (Romans 8:28). **"In this world you will have trouble. But take heart! I [Jesus] have overcome the world."** John 16:33. We also know that God uses the problems we go through to make our faith stronger (James 1:2-4).

No one wants problems, but thankfully we don't have to go through them alone. Problems can be anything from taking a test, having a fight with a friend, or losing something special to you, to bigger problems like when someone close to you dies, moving to a new city without knowing anyone, or losing a favourite pet. There will always be things that come up in life that we don't like, but God gives us **strength** when we give these hard things to Him to help us get through them.

Some of the times when I've felt closest to God was during the middle of a big problem when I had to let God comfort me and help me get through. In those times, He was my **strength** when I felt I didn't have very much. There have been so many times that God has been there for me, it's hard to pick just one to talk about.

I think one of the times God was closest to me was when my friend died when I was a teenager. He was a friend from church and my youth group. Our youth group was on a hike, and my friend got too close to the edge of the cliff. He fell and died. His name was David. I was supposed to be on the hike that day, but I got called into work, so I wasn't there when it all happened, which was a blessing because it was very traumatic for those who were there to witness it all. During that time, God was very close and near to me and my friends while we cried and went through the emotions of losing our friend. It was a comfort that I can't explain in words, just knowing that He was with me, close to me, giving me the ability to go on even during the sadness and pain of it all. It made me feel thankful that I wasn't alone, and I knew God was with me. I could feel His presence with me every day at school, at work, or wherever I went.

In the moments when I don't know what to do, I pray to God, and He carries me. It's amazing how God can be so close to us. This is something that is part of who God is, as it says in Psalm 34:18, **"The Lord is there to rescue all who are discouraged and have given up hope."** (CEV) Added to that, He is close to you when you pray and ask Him for help: **"Come close to God, and God will come close to you."** James 4:8 (NLT) These are both promises from God to you.

FEELING THE PRESSURE

Do you sometimes feel a lot of pressure? Do you feel pressure in school? Maybe you work really hard, but you feel you never get the good marks you want to. Maybe you compare yourself to your friends and how they do in school. It can be tough!

Do you feel pressure at home? Maybe you have a sibling who is great at everything, and you haven't yet found the thing that you're good at. Or maybe your parents want you to be or act a certain way, and you have a hard time doing that. It can feel like you're always letting them down.

Do you feel pressure in other areas? There are so many things in life that put pressure on us. Sadly, the wrong kind of pressure can make us do things we wouldn't normally do. It's easy to be led by our feelings and feel pressure to do things perfectly, but nothing and no one can ever be perfect other than God.

Although we have all these feelings and **emotions** inside us, it's important to not let them rule us. What do I mean by that? Say your friend wants you to wear a certain kind of clothes, but you know you wouldn't be allowed, and you don't feel comfortable wearing them. It can be easy to let your feelings tell you that you need to do what they're telling you so you'll be cool, or fit in, but if you give into your feelings, not only will you be not listening to your parents, but you could get yourself in trouble or do something you'll feel bad about later. Your feelings and your heart can often tell you two different things. Your feelings are based on **emotions**: feeling cool, fitting in, not wanting to be made fun of. But when you've surrendered to Jesus, your heart is based on the truth of knowing right from wrong. Your heart is what you should always go with because you can trust the **Holy Spirit** speaks to our hearts and helps guide us with what we should do.

When there's a lot of pressure on you, it can make you feel afraid, or even like you need to panic. Those are also **emotions** and feelings. Once you get to that point, it's hard to turn around and make wise decisions. If you notice you're becoming worried, or feeling pressure, stop and ask yourself:

•Why are you doing that thing (activity, job)?

•Is it because you're trying to please someone?

•Are you feeling overwhelmed?

To answer all those questions, if you're feeling pressure or overwhelmed, you need to stop what you're doing and practice some calming activities like reading or going for a walk. Practice and try those techniques and it should bring some calm to your mind and body.

Many times we get worked up with all the things we think we have to do. Yes, there are things we need to do, but do you have to do them right now? Are you able to put that thing aside until a later time when you feel more ready to do it? Or are there too many things on your plate, and you need to let go of one? Sometimes just stopping and practicing the calming activities above will help you to calm down, but it's also important to check in with yourself and see if you've taken on too many things. Remember, we still need to make sure we have time to rest, and spend time with God if we want to be at peace.

When you're overwhelmed your mind has a hard time keeping

up with all the things it has to do. Once you get overwhelmed, your mind isn't able to organize your thoughts properly and that's often what leads to feeling anxious.

Both lack of peace and a buildup of pressure are a recipe for anxiety. If the task doesn't need to be done immediately, put it aside until you feel you have the time and energy to give it what it needs. The time will come when you will feel ready to do it, and you will enjoy it so much more.

TAKING THE TIME YOU NEED

Have you ever had times where you would say yes to something that you knew you didn't have time for or didn't want to do, but you didn't want to say no? I used to have a hard time saying no when someone would ask me to help out, because I love to help. But I would create issues for myself if I said yes when I didn't have the time to do it.

I believe we can be like Martha, in Luke 10:38-42:

"As Jesus and his disciples were on their way, he came to a village where a woman named Martha opened her home to him. She had a sister called Mary, who sat at the Lord's feet listening to what he said. But Martha was distracted by all the preparations that had to be made. She came to him and asked, "Lord, don't you care that my sister has left me to do the work by myself? Tell her to help me!" "Martha, Martha," the Lord answered, "you are worried and upset about many things, but few things are needed—or indeed only one. Mary has chosen what is better, and it will not be taken away from her."

Just as Martha was overwhelmed with everything she thought she needed to do, we can easily take on too many things, which leads to frustration. Martha was frustrated because she believed her sister should have helped her, and worked just as hard as her. She was irritated that her sister, Mary, got to enjoy Jesus's company and teaching while she had to work. But the truth is that Martha didn't have to do any of the things she was doing. Jesus wanted her to sit with Him, too, but like we so often do, we put the pressure on ourselves to perform or do things in order to please others or sometimes because we think we will disappoint Jesus if we aren't always working. Jesus wasn't pleased by Martha's effort, even though she thought He would be. His desire was to spend time with her. The chores could wait.

It is the same for us when it comes to our time with God. He doesn't want you to worry about all the things you could do like homework, or working on a project. He just wants you to rest with

Him. He doesn't want you to put pressure on yourself to perform or be "perfect." He instead wants to spend time with you growing your faith in Him during prayer, reading the Bible, or listening to worship music. The time will come when you can get back to the things you need to do, but don't waste the special time with Jesus that you need in order to be filled by Him. If you spend time with Him and allow Him to fill you up, He will also give you the energy and ability to accomplish all that you need to do. Added to that, it's good to say no sometimes and take on only the things that you know you can do or have time for.

WHAT DO YOU BELIEVE?

As you continue working towards **courage** instead of fear, I want you to remember that you need to make a choice to believe what God says in the Bible, His promises, and the truth the **Holy Spirit** speaks to you, more than anything else. The enemy will lie to you and put thoughts in your mind that will make you question everything you think, feel, and believe.

When I really started working on taking control of my thoughts, the enemy would try to put doubts in my mind to make me question my faith. The enemy was throwing everything he could at me to see what would stick. I had to make a choice: Do I believe the thoughts popping into my mind, or do I believe the Bible? I knew that I could trust the Bible because it is truth, but I couldn't always trust my thoughts. I knew that I had to start having faith in the promises of the Bible, otherwise I would not see all that God had in store for me. I really wanted to see those promises working in my life, so I made the decision to trust the Bible more than I trusted my feelings.

God will not love you any more or any less if you don't take a step forward. His love doesn't change. He will still feel the same about you. He won't be mad at you. God is with you through this entire journey. You can trust in Him to help you and guide you. Below is a verse that is a promise from God, to you, and one that you can pray whenever you need encouragement! You aren't doing this alone. Let Him help you take that first step to freedom.

> "Fear not, for I am with you; be not dismayed, for I am your God; I will strengthen you; yes, I will help you, I will uphold you with My righteous right hand." Isaiah 41:10 (NKJV)

Ask Yourself...

1. In which areas do you feel pressure? List them. (example: in sport, at home, with friends, or schoolwork).

2. Why do you feel pressured in those areas?

3. How can you practice being more like Mary?

62

"Dear God, I ask you to help me keep going, and not give up. I also ask you to help me let go of any pressures around me. I want to spend time with you and I'm so glad that I can! Amen."

CHAPTER FIVE

How Your Thoughts Affect You

I once heard a tale about a man with two wolves. It goes like this:

An old Chief was teaching his grandson about life: "A fight is going on inside me," he said to the boy."It is a terrible fight and it is between two wolves. One is evil–he is anger, jealousy, sadness, regret, greed, full of himself, **pity,** guilt, lies, and **pride**."

He continued, "The other is good – he is joy, peace, love, hope, calm, **humility**, kindness, care, **generosity**, truth, **compassion**, and faith. The same fight is going on inside you–and inside every other person, too."

The grandson thought about it for a minute and then asked his grandfather: "Which wolf will win?"

The old Chief simply replied, "The one you feed"2

We can choose what we think about, and how much time we spend thinking about it. You can focus on the bad or the good, the fear or the peace. You can focus on kindness or on all the wrong things people have done to you. You have the option of being gentle or harsh with yourself and with others.

In the tale, the grandfather is correct in saying that there is a battle going on in all of us. That battle is good versus evil. We know that God is good, and He lives on the inside of us. The enemy, Satan, is evil, and he is constantly trying to trick us to bring us down in any way that he can.

> The thief comes only to steal and kill and destroy; I have come that they may have life, and have it to the full.
> John 10:10

When it comes to "feeding the wolf" like in our story above, we need to be careful who we decide to feed. If we want **courage** and faith, trust and hope, we need to feed the good wolf. That means choosing to think about good things, and choosing to read the Bible, and praying. It also means filling your mind with good thoughts. It's important to carefully choose what you watch on TV or the internet, as well as what you think or talk about with friends. In the Bible, the apostle Paul told us how important this is. He said in Philippians 4:8: **"Finally, brothers and sisters, whatever is true, whatever is noble, whatever is right,**

whatever is pure, whatever is lovely, whatever is admirable—
if anything is excellent or praiseworthy—think about such
things."

Paul knew the power of choosing to keep his mind on these
things. Paul wrote in Philippians 4:11, "I have learned to be
content whatever the circumstances." He also says that his
peace has nothing to do with what goes on in his life, but it has
everything to do with his thoughts. If we wait for all the things in
our life to be easy in order to be happy, then we will be waiting our
entire lives to be happy, because the things in our lives aren't
usually perfect. We have many hard situations in our lives:
friendships that go through ups and downs, stress from school or
friends, or perhaps there are hard things going on in your family.
Those things affect us all. If we allow those hard things to let us
decide how we feel, we will be **disappointed** a lot of the time.

I remember one time when I hurt myself. I was only ten or
eleven, and I had flipped off my bike and slid down a gravel hill on
my knees. When I stood up, there was blood running down my legs
and rocks had wedged themselves into my skin. We were camping
and my parents weren't around, so I had to walk back to the
campsite. It was a pretty long walk, and I was in a lot of pain, but I
noticed something interesting on my long walk back to my
campsite. When I thought about my cuts and how much it hurt, it
seemed to make my cuts hurt even more. Or if I would feel bad for

myself, that also made my cuts hurt more. But when I would instead tell myself that I was strong, I could make it to the campsite, and that I was going to be okay, it hurt less, or at least I was better able to handle it. I challenged myself to be strong, and I made it through that situation as well as many others after that. Isn't it amazing that our thoughts and our mind have so much power over how we feel?

If you are feeding the wrong wolf, the wrong thoughts are going to win.

THE PATHWAYS IN YOUR BRAIN

Think of your brain like a bunch of pathways in a field. There are wide ones, thin ones, and all kinds of other sizes in-between. Our brains create new paths each day, and this activity is called **neuroplasticity**. I know that's a big word, but what it means is that our brains are able to create new ways of thinking.

Have you ever gone dirt biking before or driven down a dirt road? The more the road has been driven or biked on, the deeper the tracks get. If they get too deep, they're very hard to get out of, and the vehicle (or the bike) has to stay in that rut. It can't get out of it because it's too deep.

Our brain makes similar pathways with our thoughts. When you think about something painful or hard from the past, your brain builds a path from that painful experience, and the more you think about it, the bigger and wider that pathway becomes. It then turns into a fear or worry. It is hard to change your thinking once you've worried about it for a long time, because that pathway to worry has become a rut, so you get stuck in that way of thinking. That's how your mind gets stuck in a loop of worry, which is why it can feel so hard to get out of that worried way of thinking.

But I have amazing news: God has created a way out for you! Neuroplasticity is the ability for your brain to change those pathways, which means you can actually fill in those **negative** thought highways, and replace them with new, **positive** highways by choosing to focus on the right things. We replace our **negative** thoughts with **positive** ones. We replace lies with the truth.

Thinking positively is going to take work because those **negative** pathways have created a pattern in your brain. The more you think about what worries you, the more direct and fast the pathway to worry is. For example, if you are worried about going to the doctor and you keep thinking about how much you're worried about it, or you think about a time when you went and didn't like it, or you think about how bad it might be, you will create a stronger worry pathway about going to the doctor. Over time, as that worry pathway is used, it will get deeper and wider and turn into a highway. But if you instead practice thinking positively about going, and replace your worry with the truth, over time that worry will begin to go away. This is one of a few key things you need to do to begin to train your brain to think the right way.

Training your brain to use new pathways will take time and practice, but you will start to notice a change. When fear first started taking over in my mind, I didn't realize I was going down the "**negative** thinking highway", but after I asked God to show me how to get out of that way of thinking, I started to be aware that I was doing it. It's a matter of replacing **negative** thoughts or worries with new, **positive** ways of looking at the situation. We will learn in the next chapter, how to apply these skills.

I want to encourage you that you **can** do this. If I can do it, you can do it too. If God can do it for me, He can do it for you. The beauty of being God's child is that we aren't doing this alone. God is here to help you and He promises that He will. The proof is in His Word, the Bible:

> No temptation has overtaken you except what is common to mankind. And God is faithful; he will not let you be tempted beyond what you can bear. But when you are tempted, he will also provide a way out so that you can **endure** it. I Corinthians 10:13

May the God of hope fill you with all joy and peace as you trust in him, so that you may overflow with hope by the power of the **Holy Spirit.** Romans 15:13

Yet the LORD longs to be gracious to you; therefore he will rise up to show you compassion. For the LORD is a God of justice. Blessed are all who wait for him. Isaiah 30:18

"Have I not commanded you? Be strong and courageous. Do not be afraid; do not be discouraged, for the LORD your God will be with you wherever you go." Joshua 1:9

In my distress I called to the LORD; I cried to my God for help. From his temple he heard my voice; my cry came before him, into his ears.
Psalm 18:6

Take delight in the LORD, and he will give you the desires of your heart.
Psalm 37:4

"Ask and it will be given to you; seek and you will find; knock and the door will be opened to you." Matthew 7:7

Read these verses as many times as you need encouragement. Write them out and put them on your wall in your room or your journal.

If the only thing you can say is, "God, show me the way out," then pray that. I read 1 Corinthians 10:13 (above) often because sometimes I don't know the answer or the way. I just know I need God's help, and each and every time I ask Him for help, He shows me the way (see Proverbs 16:9).

RELYING ON GOD'S STRENGTH

I want to be very clear: **You have a job to do, but you cannot do it in your own strength.** You need to rely on God to help, guide, and change your mind. Pray throughout the day. Remember that you can pray anytime, anywhere, and about anything!

It's so important to put what you learn into action. Let me tell you a story of how God showed me that He's taking care of me.

A few years ago, I had this weird tingling feeling in my legs for a number of weeks. I had gone to the doctor, but they weren't really sure what it was. However, God had been teaching me to trust in Him for the little and the big things. I felt that I had done all I could (by going to the doctor) and that what I needed to now do was be patient and trust in God while I waited.

I wouldn't say I enjoyed waiting on God. I wanted the solution right away, but I chose to be patient. I made a decision that I wasn't going to worry. I asked the **Holy Spirit** to help me be patient, and to keep my mind **positive**. I said, "God I trust you to take care of me, and I ask you to show me the way." I prayed that same prayer for a few days, then one day I felt God put the word "magnesium" in my mind. (Magnesium is a mineral that our body needs, like a kind of vitamin.) I was surprised and asked God what that meant, but then I felt God say to my heart again,

"Magnesium." I thought, "Well this is strange. Magnesium?" But then I remembered my prayer, and I thought maybe it was God's answer to my problem.

I decided to give it a try and that afternoon I went to the store, and I picked up some magnesium. A few hours later the funny tingling in my legs was gone. I was so thankful! I was so grateful God showed me the way. It was one of many miracles God performed in my body.

I believe He was waiting for me to let go of control, worry, and of doing it myself. Sometimes we forget that God is our doctor, He is our healer, and He is the one who takes care of us! He knows the number of hairs on our head and the way we were put together. Yes, of course we still need to see our doctor from time to time, and yes, God often works through our doctors, too, but we need to go to God first, and trust that He will lead us.

GRATITUDE

You have a choice in how you feel, based on what kinds of thoughts you're focusing on. We all have a choice to make: Either focus on the **negative,** which leads to fear, or focus on the **positive**, which leads to peace. Or we say it another way: focus on the lies, which leads to fear, or focus on the truth, which leads to peace.

Like in the tale of the two wolves, the one we feed is the one that wins. One of the mindsets that brings peace, freedom, joy, and hope is being thankful (or grateful). Look at your life and the things you can be grateful for. It will be different for everyone, but they might include your school, your friends, your family, where you live, or the hobbies you enjoy. There is so much we can be thankful for if we take the time to notice. Taking time to think about your blessings in the moment is important, **especially** when you're feeling anxious.

If you are feeling worried or anxious, remind yourself to start counting the things you're thankful for: the sound of the rain on your roof, the warm fire, the cozy blanket, your pet, or whatever that is. Doing this will **take your mind off of your worry/anxiety**, and help you to **focus on the positive**.

For me it took practice and time, and it will for you too. Pray about it anytime you worry, and practice the steps for **overcoming** it.

Ask Yourself...

1. Have you been feeding your mind with the **positive** or the **negative**? Why do you think that is?

2. How will you practice feeding your mind with **positive** things each day? Which of the verses in this chapter will you put up in your room to help remind you?

_____
_____
_____
_____
_____
_____
_____
_____
_____

"Dear God, thank
you for helping me each day.
As I learn more about freedom
from fear, please help me to practice
what I've learned as well as
remembering to be thankful for
what I have. Thank you that
all good gifts come from
you. Amen."

CHAPTER SIX

The Steps

As we've discovered, it takes time and effort to **overcome** fear and live in the peace God provides. In this chapter, we will look at the steps you need to take to get there. I find it helpful when someone gives me a clear list of steps to follow, and then my part is to follow the steps.

The first steps we will talk about are called the "The Warm Up Steps." These are meant for you to do whenever you think about them during the day or night. These steps are a bigger breakdown of the habits we talked about in Chapter 2. These can be done when you're at school, the grocery store, driving, lying in bed at night, or whenever you remember to do it. By practicing these steps you will be creating those new **positive** paths that we talked about earlier.

THE WARM UP STEPS

1. **Think about what you're thinking about.** This is something you will do often. Check in with yourself and pay attention to your thoughts. Write in a journal the thoughts from the day, paying attention to what things worried you. Write them down. If they're **negative**: don't keep thinking about the **negatives** in that situation, but instead think about it in a **positive** way. You could also choose to think about what you are thankful for. Notice the things around you, friends or family that you're thankful for, pets, or things in your room. You can write down the things you're thankful for or just say them out loud. Example: **Negative** thought: "I'm worried that at my doctor's appointment next week, I will have to get a needle." Instead think positively about it: "Whatever happens at my appointment, I can ask God to help me through it, and I know that He will." You are replacing the lie with the truth from God's word (Philippians 4:13 says, "I can do all things through Christ who gives me strength.")

2. **Find the Root.** One of the most important steps is figuring out what is at the root of your worry. For me, I had to look at what I journaled about my thoughts and see what things I was worrying about. Next I prayed and asked God to help show me

where the fear came from. Ask yourself questions like, "What made me feel this way? When did it start? Why am I worried about that?" Asking those questions will help lead you to the root cause behind your worry. This is one of the most important steps because without it, you can't identify the problem. Once you identify the root of your worry, you will replace that worry with the truth, and the truth will set you free! An example: in your journal where you write your thoughts/worries from the day, you notice you wrote down many times that you kept worrying about getting sick from kids in your class. You pray, and perhaps God puts in your heart that the root of your worry about sickness is that you don't believe God will help you through it. You have a lack of trust in God for His ability to take care of you. That is the root worry. This step can be very helpful to do with a parent or counsellor, but it can also be done on your own.

3. **Take time to pray**. It can be quick and in your heart or out loud (however you feel comfortable). Pray about your worry and ask God to help you **overcome** it and to be strong. It may seem simple to say, "Pray," but the power of prayer is amazing. You can look back on the different prayers in the yellow balloons if you're feeling stuck.

4. **Replace the lies with the truth.** In this step, you will look at the root of your worry, see what the lie is, and replace it with the truth. Using the same example above, the root of your worry is that God won't take care of you, and you don't trust Him in this. That is a lie from the enemy, so you need to replace it with the truth. If you have a Bible or are using the Bible App or even doing a search online, look up "Bible verses about God taking care of me." From that list, write down all the verses that talk about God taking care of you. (There are a lot, I promise you!) Write these down and practice reading them. Memorize them if you can. The next time the worry thought pops into your mind, replace it with the truth from those verses in the Bible. Do this for each worry. It will take practice, but it will work in an amazing way to replace those lies with the truth and give you peace. If you need help from a parent, counsellor, or friend, don't be afraid to ask.

5. **If you are able to do the thing you're worried about, do it.** That might be trying a new food, or saying hello to a new classmate. Whatever that thing is, trust God that He is with you and will give you the **strength** to do it. Don't practice this step though, until you have completed the steps above. You want to create new, **positive** thoughts around this thing, not

more fear. That's why it's important to replace the worry/lie with the truth. By believing the truth about God and His word, you will have **positive** thoughts instead of **negative** or worried thoughts. That will give you the courage to step out in faith. Practicing doing the thing that you used to worry about will help you to build **positive** feelings towards that thing, and then you'll be one step closer to **overcoming** it. Let me add to this by saying that practicing this is going to take faith. There isn't an easy way to do this. You may feel uncomfortable at first, but once you practice reminding yourself of the truth and exercise your faith, you'll be amazed at how strong and confident you feel, because when we use our faith, it's Jesus working in us. We don't do it in our own strength, we do it in Jesus' strength.

Continue the Warm Up Steps every day. Think of it like practicing an instrument or a new skill. It will take time, but soon it will become a habit. These are the steps that you'll practice all the time, whether you're anxious or not. They become the foundation (or the bottom piece) that everything else will be built on top of.

Have you ever painted something like a piece of wood or a picture? When you paint something, you have to start with the bottom coat of paint first. If it's a picture, the first layer is usually the grass or sky. That goes on before you add things like flowers, trees, or people. That's what the the Warm Up Steps are like: the bottom coat of paint. They are important for making the rest of the picture, but they have to happen first, and be practiced as often as you think of it. You don't need to think about them all the time, but practice it a couple of times a day. There's no rush and there's no perfect way to do this. Think of it like baby steps, one at a time. It will take time to train yourself to take those new **positive** highways!

IN A MOMENT OF ANXIETY

These next steps are for the times when you feel anxious. Sometimes when you're feeling anxious, there isn't an adult around to help you walk through these steps. I always encourage you to be open and share with an adult you trust if you have anxiety because they will help you through it, and be there to listen and help if needed.

You can learn and practice the steps yourself for **overcoming** anxiety. Learning on your own can build confidence and help you have peace knowing you can do it on your own. Here are the steps, for when you're feeling anxious:

THE OVERCOMING ANXIETY STEPS

1. **Pray**. It can be quick and in your heart or out loud (however you feel comfortable). Pray about your worry and ask God to help you **overcome** it, and to be strong. Remember that God is always ready to listen to whatever is on your heart and mind, and you can talk freely to Him. He doesn't judge you or think badly of you if you worry. He wants to be there to help you and comfort you. Talk to God like you would an adult or a friend; after all, you are God's friend. Mail your worries to Him like we talked about in Chapter 2. Find a little container to put them in, and once they're in there, leave them with God and focus your mind on other things.

2. **Practice replacing the lies with the truth.** Using the truth of the Bible and what God says, remind yourself of the truth. Keep those verses you found nearby in a journal, on your tablet, or written on paper and posted around your room. Keep reminding yourself of the truth, and I promise it will start to get rid of those **negative** pathways and make big, **positive** pathways.

3. **Read the book of Psalms in the Bible**. Psalms is such a special book of the Bible because it is full of the thoughts and mind of David, who was really honest with God about what he felt. Sometimes he felt really strong and **brave**, and other times

he felt worried and alone. We all go through a range of **emotions** and feelings. I believe reading what David prayed to God will bring you some peace. It's so honest and real, and it helps you to realize that you're not alone. Just like God was with David when he was being chased by an angry king who wanted to kill him, God will be with you in whatever your worry is, too.

4. **Go for a walk.** Sometimes it's nice to curl up in your bed or sit beside the fire to pray or think, but other times you may feel too worked up to sit down. That's when going for a nice walk or sitting outside in a backyard (if you have one), is a great idea. Being in nature is not only scientifically proven to be calming, but it reminds us of a God who's bigger than our problems. If you're not allowed to go outside by yourself, come up with a plan with an adult before so that you know what you are allowed to do if the time comes.

God created us to have thoughts, feelings and **emotions**, but when you're in the middle of feeling anxious, you are not able to think clearly. Later, when you're calm, your mind is more able to think situations through. When you're calm is a good time to talk to your parents or an adult that you trust about how you're feeling about something that's worrying you, and it's also a good time to come up with a plan about what to do if you're feeling anxious. If you do that when you're calm, you can often talk through a really good solution that you can both work on together to **overcome** the anxiety.

Sometimes we need the help of doctor or counsellor who knows a lot about these kinds of things. You never need to feel bad if that's what needs to happen for you. Remember what we talked about earlier, that God very often works through the doctors in order to help us. Sometimes that's just what we need, and God will help you find just the right doctor for you. Do what the doctor or counsellor tells you to do, and always remember that God loves you, and you **will** get through this together! Believe that God is taking care of you and will help you as you give Him your trust and time. Also, remember that whether you're going to see a counsellor or not, you should always pray and ask God to help you.

In each situation, it doesn't matter what the worry is; God can handle it, and He will work to bring all things together for your good (see Romans 8:28, John 14:13).

Once you surrender yourself and your will and give it all to God, the worry and anxiety will lift.

I have to work at surrendering to God every day. I also always pray for God to renew my mind. Ask God to show you where you can trust Him more. Pray, and the **Holy Spirit** will show you.

Each day you are one step closer to walking in peace of mind than the day before. Remember what it says in 2 Corinthians 4:16, **"Therefore we do not lose heart. Though outwardly we are wasting away, yet inwardly we are being renewed day by day."** We can hope and trust in the fact that God is taking us through this journey, and that we are never alone. Don't look ahead at how far you have to go, but instead be proud of how far you've come. Walking towards freedom is a **day by day** effort. Set your mind on God, and let the **Holy Spirit** do the work He will do in and through you.

Remember, the Warm Up Steps are:

1. Think about what you're thinking about
2. Find the root
3. Take time to pray
4. Replace the lies with the truth
5. If you're able to do thing you're worried about, do it

The Overcoming Anxiety Steps are:

1. Pray
2. Practice replacing the lies with the truth
3. Read the book of Psalms
4. Go for a walk

Ask Yourself...

1. How will changing your thinking pathways help you **overcome** anxiety?

2. How will you make sure to practice the Warm Up Steps daily?

"Dear God, I know you will give me the skills and abilities to overcome this anxiety, and I ask you, Holy Spirit, to speak to me and encourage me along the way. I know that I can do all things through you! Amen."

CHAPTER SEVEN

Do the Things You're Afraid Of

Have you ever done something you were afraid of doing, then tried it and realized it wasn't nearly as scary as you thought it would be? I remember the first time I went on a fast ride at the fair. I was really scared to go because I figured I would get sick or be scared on the ride. My friends kept encouraging me to try it, so finally I took a brave step forward and tried out the ride. I was so nervous beforehand, but my friends kept encouraging me while we waited for the ride to start up. Finally, it began and started to rock back and forth, and I felt even more nervous. But once the ride was going, I realized it wasn't actually scary at all. I had built it up in my mind beforehand, and rather than being scared, I was having a blast! When I got off the ride, I ran to get in line for the next ride. I was hooked! That taught me a lesson that day that we can easily build things up in our minds that we aren't sure about. New things can feel scary if we let them, or we can look at them as new adventures. The choice is ours!

It's really neat that we have the ability to make our own choices about what we do. Even though your mind may tell you you're afraid, you can still choose to do that thing because you get to make that choice! Many times when we think we will be afraid of something, like a new food or a ride at the fair, we try it, and it's not nearly as scary as we thought. We may even end up enjoying it!

When I talk about doing something you're afraid of, I am not talking about doing something foolish like walking up to a strange dog and saying, "I don't want to be afraid of dogs anymore, so I'll walk up to a strange dog and hope it doesn't bite me." That would be a foolish thing to do. What I am saying is if you are feeling fear in an area that you know is safe to try, like trying a new food or inviting someone new to play with you, let God help you **overcome** it, even if your feelings feel different. When you follow the steps above, you will replace those worried thoughts with **positive** ones that will give you the courage to **overcome** your fear. You can begin facing your fears with faith and courage. It's important to follow all of the steps in order, rather than just picking a few to try because each step was created to give you success.

PUSHING YOURSELF TO CONQUER FEAR

An example would be someone like Annie. Annie is a real person, and this is her story: Annie was afraid of flying in an airplane and leaving home. Many of her fears about it were based on **unrealistic** worries. She knew that in reality there was a very low chance of a plane crash, and that she would be fine if she was away from home, but her fears always took over her mind. When she travelled with her family, she didn't enjoy the travel part, and she was worried the whole time.

As she learned more about trusting in God and understanding the root cause of where her fear came from, she began to trust in God more, and she was able to start taking baby steps towards doing it while she was still nervous. It was definitely hard, and it took practice and **determination**, but what she started to notice was that when she took the little baby steps, she was okay! The next time she had to take another step, it was easier than the last time; and, step by step, it became easier to have courage, and not be afraid. That was the freedom she began to notice, and that same freedom is possible for you, too!

As she grew in her faith and stepped forward, she noticed that fear was going away in other areas of her life too, but they all started with baby steps. For example, at the beginning, she would take the baby step of going on a day trip with her family a few hours away from home. Once she realized she was okay, she would have a lot of fun. That built a little more faith in her for the next time and the next chance she had to face fear. After a while, God gave her the ability to travel in airplanes with no fear. He was faithful and kept speaking truth to her, and before long, she was no longer afraid to fly in airplanes or travel. Being **brave** helped build her trust in God, knowing He was taking care of her. If she hadn't taken those first baby steps, she would likely still be afraid today.

The important thing I want to make clear is that you **will have to be uncomfortable some of the time,** mostly at the beginning. Using your faith and pushing away fear doesn't come easily, but God will help you! Your job is to trust God no matter how afraid you feel. It may not feel good, but that's when you pray, and trust God anyway. He will show up by giving you the **courage** to do it, and He will help you through it. He will bless you, and lead you down the path to freedom. Being **brave** while being **uncomfortable** in the beginning will help you to **overcome** your fear in the long run!

In my faith journey, I want to grow every day in trusting God. I want to grow in **courage** and **strength**, but those are not formed inside of us during the easy times, they're formed during hard times. Did you know that a diamond is formed only when there's enough pressure around it to force it into a diamond? Diamonds are not made without pressure, and look at how strong and beautiful a diamond is. Diamonds are one of the strongest rocks in the world! I think God gives us examples like that in nature so that we can see them as examples in our own lives. Just like a diamond is formed under pressure, the qualities of **strength**, **bravery**, and pushing forward are formed under pressure, through the hard times in life. The only way to get those qualities is to push yourself, even if it's only a small step.

Pushing yourself to conquer fear is important, but before you begin taking those steps, it's important to first work through figuring out the root of the fear, and practicing the steps in Chapter 6. Once you've begun replacing those **negative**/fearful thoughts with **positive**/truthful ones, you are in a healthy position to walk that out by doing the things you used to be afraid of. Practicing the steps first, helps renew your mind and gives you the courage you need to take those steps with faith, not fear.

If you think of a storm or a tornado, the last place you want to be is inside of it. You want to stay as far away as you can, but if you happen to get stuck in the middle of a storm, would it make sense to stay there in the middle of the storm, or would it make more sense to walk your way out of the storm? Staying parked in the middle of a storm doesn't get you out of it any faster, but if you can instead put one foot in front of the other, you can start to walk out of the storm. As Christians, one of the most beautiful gifts we have is we don't have to walk through these storms of life alone. God is right there with us, giving us the ability, if we only trust Him. He will walk with us, out of the storm.

EXERCISING THE COURAGE MUSCLE

As you begin to learn how to do things while you're not yet comfortable, you will start the journey of **overcoming** anxiety, but it won't always be easy. You have to make up your mind that you're going to do what it takes, even if it's hard.

Overcoming anxiety is like working out a muscle. If you lift something heavy, the first time, it's not too hard. You may begin lifting it up and down, and the first few times you do that, it's not too hard; but as you keep going, the fourth, fifth and sixth time, it gets harder and harder. You will feel a little burn in your muscles. What's happening is you're creating tiny, little tears in your muscle, and those little tears are what cause the burning feeling, but it's also how you make your muscle grow. If you stop lifting the weight when it feels hard, on that third lift, you will not build those muscles. The next time you pick up that same weight, and get to the third lift, it will not be any easier than the first time. You could pick up that same weight each day, for a year, and it will be just as hard on day 300, as it was on day one. It won't get any easier because you haven't built any muscle.

Instead, if you push past that third lift, and go up to four, eight, or ten lifts in the beginning, you begin to build stronger muscle. You won't be able to go from four lifts to forty lifts overnight, but over time you will build more and more muscle, and each time you push yourself past that burn, you will be that much stronger. Before long, you will be able to lift heavier and heavier weights.

That is what it's like to push through anxiety, and begin to **overcome** it. If you shrink back and don't push forward when you try doing the thing you're afraid of, it is like stopping the weight at the third lift. You aren't pushing yourself to face it. You aren't doing anything to push past the fear. You are staying stuck in the middle of it. Instead, if you take a step (even if it's only one step) you've now grown that '**courage** muscle' a little bit, and if each time you feel fear you push yourself just a little bit further, before you know it, that big, scary fear becomes nothing but a wimpy little weight. What used to feel really heavy will begin to feel light. The more lifts you do, and the more times you step out in faith and **courage**, the more you build those muscles. Things that were once huge worries in your life are easier. Fears that felt like mountains before are now only tiny bumps in the road that you can step over, and be on your way.

Peace is that way, too. The more you step out in **courage**, the more it builds peace, because peace is really trust in God. It may seem backward to believe that doing something that worries you will give you peace, but it will. It won't happen right away, but as you take those steps you will build **courage**, and that **courage** will help you see that you can **overcome** fear, which leads to peace.

THE BOY WHO OVERCAME FEAR

Once upon a time in an Ethiopian village, there lived a boy who was so shy and fearful of the world around him that his family called him Miobe, frightened one.

"Why do you call me that?" the boy asked his grandfather.

The old man laughed. "Because you are afraid," he answered. The boy's grandmother, his mother, his father, and the neighbors said the same thing. Miobe pondered these words and decided he must find a way to conquer fear, and that night when everyone was fast asleep, he packed a sack and set off into the world to find out what he feared and to conquer it.

He fell asleep wrapped in his blanket, but at midnight the wolves began to howl. The sound woke Miobe, but instead of running away, he walked toward the sound, saying aloud, "I will conquer you, fear."

One of the elders in the village told Miobe, "Our village is being threatened by a monster up on the mountain."

Miobe followed the old man's gaze to the top of the mountain.

"See him, there," the old man said.

"Look," said another man. "It has the head of a crocodile. A monstrous crocodile!"

"And his body is as horrible as a hippopotamus. A gigantic hippopotamus!"

"It's like a dragon!" another man cried, "with fire shooting from its snout!"

Now Miobe began to see the monster. He began to see the smoke and fire, the wrinkled skin, the fiery eyes. "I see," he said, but silently he promised himself he would not be afraid. So he walked away from the elders, into the village.

Finally Miobe decided it was up to him to destroy the monster. "I wish to conquer fear," he announced, "and so I shall go slay the monster!"

At the base of the mountain, he looked up and felt a chill of fear run down his spine. That monster looked even bigger and fierier than any dragon, fiercer than a whole pack of wolves or a nest of snakes. He remembered the days when he had been afraid. He took a deep breath and began to climb.

As he climbed, he looked up, but now he saw the monster seemed to be growing smaller.

"How strange," he said aloud. "My eyes are playing tricks on me."

He continued to climb.

"The closer I get, the smaller he looks," Miobe said confused. He continued to climb, though now he pulled his dagger from his sack so that he would be prepared.

As he came around a bend in the path, he saw the peak of the mountain before him. He gasped. The monster had disappeared.

Miobe turned and looked behind him. Surely the creature was going to sneak up from behind to attack. But when he turned, he saw nothing. He heard nothing. He held his breath. He looked left. He looked right. Suddenly he heard a sound at his feet. He looked down and saw a little creature, just like a toad with wrinkled skin and round, frightened eyes.

He bent down and picked it up. "Who are you?" he asked. "How did you become so small?" But the tiny monster said nothing, and so he cradled it in his hand and walked down the mountain.[3]

This story is a great example of facing your fears and not running away from them. The more we face our fears, the smaller they become. Miobe knew that the only way to be brave was to step forward when he felt afraid. If he didn't step forward, he would never grow in courage. The funny thing is the more he pushed himself to be brave, the smaller his fear became. The same is true for us. If you don't step out and do the things you're afraid of, you will eventually become more and more afraid of things, but instead if you push yourself to step out a little bit at a time, you will grow your 'courage muscle' and you will become more and more brave as you exercise it. Would you rather be afraid, or **overcome** it?

EXPECTING THE WORST

It can be easy to **assume** something without knowing if it's true. For example, there are times when something feels true, but you don't actually know if it is. Your feelings can make you believe something that's not true.

Think about a time when you've thought you were right about something, but it turned out you were wrong, and you got all worked up about it only to find out that what you thought wasn't actually true.

It's easy to do that in friendships sometimes. Have you ever had a time where you thought a friend was upset with you or avoiding you? Maybe you went to play with them at school recess and couldn't find them. You assumed they were playing with someone else. Then maybe later that day you tried to find them to partner up with in class, and they were already partners with someone else. Then after school you asked if they wanted to come over and hang out, and they already had plans with someone else. If you were letting your feelings guide you, you may feel like they didn't want to hang out with you, but what actually happened was different: They couldn't play at lunch because they had to go to the office for a phone call. They weren't able to partner up with you because the teacher put your friend with a student who needed help. After school your friend couldn't play because their mom decided to invite the new neighbours over to welcome them to the neighbourhood. None of those things had anything to do with your friend not wanting to hang out with you, but it could have looked that way if you let your feelings and thoughts get out of control. It's so easy to do this. We don't always **assume** the best, but with practice we can learn how.

Sometimes when our feelings or thoughts are always on our

minds, it's easy for Satan to come along and try and place even more worrying thoughts in your mind.

God can open our eyes to the lies of Satan, and we can move forward in the freedom that God offers! By taking one step at a time, God begins taking away the fear, and you will feel **peace.** It is then that we can see with open eyes the beauty of the truth: God is taking care of us, and we can put our trust and hope in Him. God doesn't do anything before we are ready. His timing is perfect and He knows when we are ready to face it. Remember, you aren't ever doing it on your own. God will help you **overcome** your fear! Pray and ask Him, and trust He is with you.

> There is a time for everything, and a season for every activity under the heavens. Ecclesiastes 3:1

Take that beautiful promise as a sign from God that if He's putting it on your heart to pray about what is causing your fear, now is the time to pray and talk to a parent, teacher, counsellor, or any adult or friend you feel comfortable with in your life. You are stronger than you think! There's grace for you in this moment because He gives us the grace we need at the time we need it. He wants you to be free, so start learning how to take those steps, today!

Ask Yourself...

1. What are some of the things you worry about?

2. Pick one from the list and write down how you will practice being **brave** in that area.

_____

_____

_____

_____

_____

_____

_____

_____

_____

_____

_____

"Dear God, I ask you to help me to think positively, and I ask that you would give me courage to be brave. I know that my courage comes from you. I also give you my worries and fears. I praise you that You are good and love me. Thank you God. Amen."

CHAPTER EIGHT

Practice and You'll Succeed

You are well on your way to **overcoming** fear! You have learned truth from the Bible, and can apply those steps to your daily life.

You've learned about:

- the power of thoughts
- the power of the Holy Spirit guiding you
- the importance of thankfulness
- neuroplasticity - the way our brains can change for the better
- steps you can practice to help overcome anxiety

All of these tools will help you in the journey you're on. I am proud of you for starting this journey and working together with the **Holy Spirit** to **overcome** fear. I believe that you want change, and God is giving you the tools you need to **overcome** anxiety. Everyone desires to be free in their lives and minds, but not everyone will do the work to have freedom.

> Now the Lord is the Spirit, and where the Spirit of the Lord is, there is freedom. 2 Corinthians 3:17

> So if the Son [Jesus] sets you free, you will be free indeed. John 8:36

God wants a life for you that's exciting, joyful, and free. Living in worry and fear creates anxiety and holds you back from a free life. I know you don't want to live this way anymore, and today could be the first day of your new way of living. Today can be first day where you take a step forward, and begin to walk in freedom.

Make today the day you stand up and say, "No more fear. No more panic. No more living in the past. I am looking forward to the future and my future is bright! I am going to do this. I **can** do this. God is with me and He is for me!"

We are not in charge, but God is. He won't give up on you. He won't leave you in your mess. He will gently encourage you many times. It could be in obvious ways, or it could be through the encouragement of a Bible verse, something your parent says, or through a friend. Either way, don't ignore His voice.

There's a reason you decided to read this book. There's reason you were led to begin this journey. He's asking you to trust Him, and let Him help you through this. After all, who's better for the job than God? He is our Shepherd, which means He takes care of us.

Jesus tells the story in the Bible about a Shepherd. The shepherd had 100 sheep and one of the sheep was lost. He left the 99 sheep in safety to go after the one who was lost, to make sure that sheep was safe (see Matthew 18:12-14). In that story, Jesus is the Shepherd, and that one sheep is you. He will always keep helping you. He wants you to be free.

PRACTICE, PRACTICE, PRACTICE

Remember to keep doing the steps, even if you think you don't need to anymore or want to give up. Those **courage** muscles will begin to grow and build up, and before long what used to be hard will become easier. You can begin running and jumping over the old way of thinking and moving into the new life that God has for you.

Continue to practice being aware of your thoughts. It takes

practice. Some areas may be harder to **overcome** than others, but that doesn't mean you should give up. You will reach victory, and it does get easier.

The areas that were once very hard for me to **overcome**, are now much easier than when I first began. If I begin to feel my mind drifting towards the past or to thoughts that aren't **positive**, I practice the steps outlined above. God has always been faithful to help me along, and He will be faithful to you as well.

If you mess up and feel you've gone backwards, don't feel let down. It means Satan is testing you by trying to tempt you and trying to get you to think you can't do it, but don't believe his lies, because God is stronger, and He is helping you win!

There is one last thing I'd like to share with you: **Faith can move mountains.** Think about that for a minute. Jesus said in Matthew 17:20, **"For truly I say to you, if you have faith the size of a mustard seed, you will say to this mountain, 'Move from here to there,' and it will move; and nothing will be impossible to you."** (also see Mark 11:23 NASB). That's a promise and it's true. I have never prayed for a mountain to move, but if God wanted me to pray for that, and that was His will, I have no doubt He could do it! Do you have faith that God can do whatever He says He can? If you trust in Him fully, you will see Him do big things in your life, including **overcoming** anxiety.

I have faith that God can do anything, and we would be powerless to stop it. He is in control. He can move actual mountains. He can turn day into night, and night into day. His power is so big and so wide, but we often forget just how powerful He is.

God has given us the amount of faith we need, it says in Romans 12:3, and when we connect that to the verse in Matthew about our faith moving mountains, I am reminded that our faith (your faith) can do anything because our God can do anything.

God is at work, even when we don't see or feel it, and when we believe with faith He continues to work, and it encourages us. Keep holding on above anything else you think or feel, because your faith in God is powerful!

An example of this is the story of Daniel in the Bible. We read in Daniel 10 that Daniel was praying to God, and asking Him to send help because he needed it. As he prayed, he didn't see anything happen, but he kept praying and hoping in faith. It says he prayed every day for twenty-one days and did not see any help. An angel came to him on day twenty-one, and the angel gave him the message that he was sent when Daniel first prayed that first day, but there was a dark force in the angel's way and he could not get to Daniel. For twenty-one days the angel kept trying to fight this darkness to get to Daniel. The angel then called upon a stronger angel, Michael, who is a warrior angel. Michael defeated the dark force, and then the first angel was able to make it to Daniel to help him. Daniel had to keep praying, and hoping in faith, and we must do the same. Daniel didn't see the results of his prayers for twenty-one days, but he kept on trusting and praying.

You may find it hard, or you may not feel like practicing these steps in the first few days. You may not feel or see that they are helping at first, but if you can keep hoping (1 Timothy 6:12), and staying strong in your faith, and trusting that God **is** at work, you will be rewarded. Watch the chains of anxiety fall off, and begin to walk in the freedom He brings! I'll say it again: **YOU CAN DO THIS!** God is on your side; He is there to fight your battles and lead you into victory! All it takes is the first step.

Ask Yourself...

1. Who may try to make you think you want to give up or think it's too hard to overcome anxiety?

2. Who can you talk to about your new plan for overcoming anxiety?

_____
_____
_____
_____
_____
_____
_____
_____
_____
_____
_____
_____
_____

"Dear God, thank you for leading me on this journey to freedom. I know that with you, all things are possible. I ask for your courage to rule in my mind and that you would help me be strong. I am excited to see what you have in store for me. I love you, God. Amen."

Glossary[1]

assume: to take for granted or without proof

bravery/brave: ready to face pain or danger; courageous

convinced: to believe or accept

courage: the ability to face fear or danger; bravery

determination: doing something without quitting, even when it's hard

disappointed: feeling let down, something worse than what you expected

emotions: a strong feeling such as joy, hatred, sorrow, or fear. There are no bad emotions, but some are harder than others

endure: to continue to the end even though it's hard

especially: more than usual

foundation: the bottom of a structure that holds up a building from beneath

fruit of the Spirit: The gifts that God has put inside of us: love, joy, peace, patience, goodness, kindness, faithfulness, gentleness, and self-control.

Holy Spirit: member of the Trinity and fully God. He is our helper, and He lives inside of us. He is the one who helps guide our thoughts, decisions, and what we know to be wrong or right.

impress: to make someone proud of you

miraculous/miracle: something that seems impossible to our ability, but God does it

negative: a bad, unwelcome, or unpleasant thing

overcome/overcoming: to win against, to get over it

overwhelming: when you feel overloaded or heavy with too much of something.

repent: asking God to forgive you for your sins, allowing Him to change your heart so you can change your behaviour so you don't do it again

strength: being strong

Trinity: God (the Father), Jesus (the Son), and the Holy Spirit (the Helper), working together as one, each member is fully God.

uncomfortable: not being comfortable

unrealistic: very unlikely to happen

weaknesses: feeling weak

Endnotes

1. "Children's, Intermediate and Advanced Online English Dictionary & Thesaurus." Wordsmyth, https://kids.wordsmyth.net/we/?ent=uncomfortable.

2. Graham, Billy. **Holy Spirit**: Activating God's Power in Your Life. Word Pub., 1988.

3. "Tell Me A Story: Conquering Fear (an Ethiopian Folk Tale)." Recordonline.com, Recordonline.com, 21 Oct. 2011, https://www.recordonline.com/article/20111024/LIFE/110240304.

Manufactured by Amazon.ca
Bolton, ON